THE LITTLE BOOK OF
MICHAEL JORDAN

First published in 2025 by OH
An Imprint of HEADLINE PUBLISHING GROUP LIMITED

1

Disclaimer:

Cataloguing in Publication Data is available from the British Library

ISBN 978-1-03542-245-6

Compiled and written by: David Clayton
Editorial: Matt Tomlinson
Designed and typset in Avenir by: Andy Jones
Project manager: Russell Porter
Production: Marion Storz
Printed and bound in China

Headline's policy is to use papers that are natural,
renewable and recyclable products and made from
wood grown in well-managed forests and other
controlled sources. The logging and manufacturing
processes are expected to conform to the
environmental regulations of the country of origin.

HEADLINE PUBLISHING GROUP LIMITED
An Hachette UK Company
Carmelite House, 50 Victoria Embankment, London EC4Y 0DZ

The authorised representative in the EEA is Hachette Ireland, 8 Castlecourt Centre,
Dublin 15, D15 XTP3, Ireland (email: info@hbgi.ie)

www.headline.co.uk   www.hachette.co.uk

THE LITTLE BOOK OF
MICHAEL
JORDAN

IN HIS OWN WORDS

UNOFFICIAL AND UNAUTHORIZED

CONTENTS

INTRODUCTION

Quite simply, Michael Jordan is one of the greatest sportsmen of all time. Even that doesn't do him justice, though, as he's also a legend off the court too. His story is both inspirational and aspirational, rising from humble beginnings to quickly prove himself and win fans in college. Fuelled by a ferocious work ethic, and brimming with natural talent, Jordan continued to rise higher and higher.

Drafted as the number three overall pick in the league by the Chicago Bulls in 1984, he soon became one of the most recognisable players in the league, known for his distinctive playing style and appetite for winning. Jordan led the Bulls to six NBA championship titles, becoming a genuine superstar along the way before calling time on a glorious career after 15 years… even if it wasn't all without drama.

Jordan's skillset on the court was matched by his business acumen off it. His momentous deal with Nike in 1984 to produce the now-iconic

Air Jordan sneaker changed the world of sports-wear endorsement forever... and made Jordan a billionaire along the way.

Add that to the lead role in one of the biggest movies of the 1990s, *Space Jam*, and a smash-hit Netflix documentary, *The Last Dance*, and it's clear that we may never see another sport star quite like Michael Jordan.

Whatever his achievements off-court, it is in basketball where his star shone brightest, with his remarkable stats and achievements, his ability to win games almost single-handedly, and, of course, that gift of soaring through the air in a superhuman way.

Jordan has been an inspiration to a generation of basketball stars, but, despite his ability to almost fly, his feet – in Air Jordans, of course – have always remained firmly on the ground.

Chapter 1

Tunnel Vision

To begin with, Michael Jordan wasn't
viewed as anything special at all.

But his self-belief, the grounding his
family gave him, and a God-given
talent soon changed the minds of
the doubters...

Tunnel Vision

I was born with a nosebleed and my parents were worried that there was something wrong with me. Later on, when I was a baby, I fell behind my parents' bed and almost suffocated. Then, when I was about two years old, I picked up two wires next to a car my father was working on. It had been raining and, again according to my father, the shock sent me flying about three feet.

Michael recounts a childhood littered with close calls, *For the Love of the Game: My Story*, 1998.

"

My father pulled me aside that summer and he said, 'Look, you don't look like you're headed in the right direction. If you want to go about doing all this mischievous stuff, you can forget sports.' That's all I needed to hear. It was like from that point on, it was tunnel vision.

"

Michael recalls a pivotal talk with his father, James, *The Last Dance*, Netflix, 2020.

He had to spend the entire day sitting and studying in my car. And I parked where I could regularly look out the window to check on him, and make sure he was there working on his studies.

Deloris Jordan

Michael's mom recounts the time her son was briefly suspended for tackling a school bully—twice! Nypost.com, April 2023.

66

One summer, my mom said, 'You just got to work,' and she got me a job as a maintenance man in a hotel. Man, I quit that job so quick! I just couldn't do it; I could not keep regular hours. It just wasn't me.

99

Michael's destiny was never hotel maintenance, *GQ*, March 1989.

Tunnel Vision

66

I was a nobody. And he was better than me. People knew him before they knew me.

99

On how his friend—the 6' 7" Leroy Smith—got in the 1978 Laney High School varsity team ahead of him in ninth grade. He vowed to never allow that to happen again, GQ, March 1989.

"

I'm going to show you—nobody
will ever work as hard as I work.

"

His pledge to his coach that the varsity setback
would be a one-off, cnbc.com, April 2020.

66

If you want to bring out the best in Michael, tell him he can't do something.

99

James Jordan

Michael's father learns reverse psychology worked wonders for his son, bbc.co.uk, May 2020.

"

I was so nervous my hands were sweating. I saw all these All-Americans and I thought I was just the lowest thing on the totem pole. Here I was, a country boy from Wilmington. But the more I played, the more confident I became. I thought to myself, 'Maybe I can play with these guys.'

"

On discarding his feelings of inferiority at his first basketball camp, ncaa.com, March 2022.

Tunnel Vision

At North Carolina, when they recruited me and asked me to attend the university, it was an opportunity to prove myself. Up to that point, everybody had heard that this kid is pretty good, but we don't know how good. He came from a small town. He wasn't preseason All-American. He wasn't in the top 100 high school kids. He didn't attend AAU games, and he was not a ranked player in the nation.

On his chance to prove himself, cigaraficionado.com, August 2005.

"

Everybody in Wilmington expected me to go to North Carolina, sit on the bench for four years, then go back to Wilmington and work at the local gas station.

"

On the low expectations of his hometown, *GQ*, March 1989.

I never thought I'd be able to play at a Division I school. Nobody from my high school ever had before. It really shocked me when North Carolina started recruiting me. I never thought that could happen.

"

On breaking new ground, ncaa.com, March 2022.

“

Whenever I was working out and got tired and figured I ought to stop, I'd close my eyes and see that list in the locker room without my name on it, and that usually got me going again.

”

On how being cut from the high-school team continued to motivate him for a long time after, espn.com.

❝

I'm the tallest. My father's about
5′ 10″, my mother's about 5′ 5″,
everybody else about 5′ 6″ or 5′ 7″.
The milkman's about 6′ 7″.

❞

Joking about where his height came from,
Late Show with David Letterman, 1989.

"

I always wanted to be tall. I thought 6' 8" inches would be nice.

"

The 6' 6" MJ on almost reaching his target height!
ncaa.com, March 2022.

Tunnel Vision

"

I had a great time in college.
It was the first time I'd been away
from home. I'd met new people
and made new friends. It was an
exciting time. It was just fun.

"

On making friends, cigaraficionado.com,
August 2005.

"

In college, I never realized the opportunities available to a pro athlete. I've been given the chance to meet all kinds of people, to travel and expand my financial capabilities, to get ideas and learn about life, to create a world apart from basketball.

"

On trying new experiences, cigaraficionado.com, August 2005.

Tunnel Vision

66

The University of North Carolina really gave me the foundation that it took to become a basketball player. Up to then, I hadn't been spoiled by the media spotlight. I was still raw. As a result, I had an appetite to prove to everybody that I was a decent basketball player, or a good enough basketball player to be at North Carolina. That was by far the purest experience for me, and the most satisfying.

99

On his happy college days, cigaraficionado.com, August 2005.

"

That turned my name from Mike to Michael Jordan. It gave me the confidence that I needed to start to excel at the game of basketball. **"**

Michael recalls how the now-legendary game-winning jump shot in the victory over the Georgetown Hoyas to win the 1982 national championship with North Carolina Tar Heels kickstarted his career, *The Last Dance*, Netflix, 2020.

66

To tell the truth, I didn't see it go in.
I didn't want to look.

99

MJ recalls THAT winning shot and admits
even he couldn't watch it, tarheeltimes.com,
March 2023.

"

I was thinking the game might come down to a last-second shot. I saw myself taking it and hitting it.

"

Picturing the moment against Georgetown helped when it all become real—and exactly as he had planned it, history.com, October 2021.

He has talent. He's a very quick learner. He's a bright student, which passes on to the court, and a remarkable young man who has fit in extremely well.

Dean Smith

The North Carolina coach is effusive in his praise of MJ on December 26, 1981, talksport.com, March 2021.

"

He truly has no flaws, or so few they aren't worth mentioning. He has great jumping ability and a classic jump shot. He can handle the ball on the break. He can do it all. **"**

Journalist

An unattributed journalist reports on Michael Jordan's college progress, *Los Angeles Times*, 1983

.

Michael is a late bloomer. He improves every month. Look at his defense. When he was a freshman, he had a lot of work to do. Last year, he won the defensive award 12 times. He's going to be one of our great defensive players, although I don't think I'll tell him that until he graduates. But you can just watch him get better and better. When he was a freshman, he ran the 40 in 4.8 (seconds). This year, he ran it in 4.3.

Dean Smith

MJ's coach on Jordan's progress in 1983, ncaa.com, March 2022.

"

It was Coach [Dean] Smith's call. I relied so much on his knowledge. The NBA was an area where I wasn't too knowledgeable. My parents weren't knowledgeable about it, either. And it was a great opportunity. Coach Smith felt that it would be the best opportunity for me to make it in professional basketball. Once he researched the situation to find out where I would go in the draft, then I started weighing the pros and cons.

"

Coach Smith knew he was working with a special talent so convinced MJ to enter the NBA draft for 1984 and miss his senior year at college…
sportsrush.com, October 2023.

I haven't bitten it off yet. **"**

Dean Smith

The coach's attempts to get Michael to keep his tongue in his mouth when he played were falling on deaf ears, ncaa.com, March 2022.

66
He was the perfect guy for me. He kept me humble, but he challenged me. 99

On the influential Coach Smith, biography.com, June 2020.

Tunnel Vision

> "He's a perfect player. When I grew up, I wanted to be 6' 7" and I wanted to be able to do anything on the court. I wanted to grow up to be what Michael Jordan grew up to be."

Matt Doherty
Former North Carolina teammate on Michael Jordan, ncaa.com, March 2022.

66

You must expect great things
of yourself before you can
do them.

99

On achieving success, inc.com, April 2016.

"

To learn to succeed, you must first learn to fail.

"

On learning from failure, medium.com,
June 2022

66

If you accept the expectations
of others, especially negative ones,
then you never will change the
outcome.

99

On challenging expectations, thebookofman.com.

Tunnel Vision

I decided to turn pro in 1984, right after I finished my junior season at the University of North Carolina. I went to the Chicago Bulls as the number three draft pick. My attitude going into training camp as a rookie was to impress.

On a keen start, *Vanity Fair*, October 1998.

"

If Portland had won the coin flip, they would have taken Hakeem, and I would have ended up in Houston. But the coin flip came up Houston, and that put me back to third with Chicago.

"

A coin flip at the NBA draft and destiny edges MJ towards the Bulls, cigaraficionado.com, August 2005.

Chapter 2

*I Believe
I Can Fly...*

Michael Jordan has joined the
Chicago Bulls and his determination
to be the best means practice,
practice, practice, and it isn't long
before all that talent and self-belief
sees him soar...

All I can say is that the people in Chicago are in for a real treat.

Bernard King

New York Knicks small forward on Michael's Chicago Bulls drafting in 1984, wttw.com

66
I hate to lose. I guess that's it as much as anything.

99

On his drive for success, ncaa.com,
March 2022.

“

Bird was showing me it was all business now, and I was beneath him. I didn't forget.

”

As MJ took part in a series of Olympic warm-ups for the U.S.A. against NBA All-Stars, Boston Celtics legend Larry Bird kicks a ball back over the young pretender's head as he went to retrieve it rather than handing it to the young star, sportsrush.com, January 2023.

The Facts #1

Michael Jordan signed with Nike in 1984 at the advice of his agents and parents, having initially wanted to join Adidas. He would receive $550,000 per year over five years. In the first year of the contract, the company sold $126 million-worth of Jordan-related product.

"

I didn't go out and buy cars and clothes like rookies today. I always tried to dress nice, but I never wanted to be the best-dressed. Not even close. I lived very modestly. Away from the game I wanted to fit in. But on the court I was all business. I wanted to stand out.

"

On his modesty off-court, *Vanity Fair*, October 1998.

"

I wanted to impress my teammates,
my coaches, the owners—everybody.
I wanted them to say, 'This kid is special.
This kid has the right mind, the right skills,
the right motivation.' All my effort that first
year was geared toward proving myself.
I went as hard as I could all the time.
I tried to win every drill, every scrimmage.
I tried to dominate, but never vocally. I felt
until I earned the right to speak I wasn't
going to say a word.

"

On working hard, *Vanity Fair*, October 1998.

66

Failure makes me work even harder.

99

More inspiration, inc.com, April 2016.

The Facts #2

Michael Jordan was named the 1984–85 NBA Rookie of the Year. He finished his first season with the Chicago Bulls starting all 82 games with a stat line of 28.2 points per game, 6.5 rebounds per game and a .515 field goal percentage.

Because I was taught that a hurt dog'll holler, always. If they are going to be mad at me because I'm trying to lead a positive life, then I must be steppin' on some very soft toes there.

Michael recalls being unimpressed with some of his teammates' partying during his rookie year and how he turned his back on drugs and alcohol to focus on his career, *GQ*, March 1989.

"

I wouldn't say it's an addiction, but it's a passion. When you have a passion, you want to do it as much as possible. Addiction means you can't help yourself. I have a strong passion for the game of basketball.

"

On the crucial difference between addiction and passion, cigaraficionado.com, August 2005.

The Facts #3

A famous moment from Jordan's early career was on August 26, 1985, when Jordan shocked the arena during an exhibition game in Trieste, Italy, by shattering the glass of the backboard with a dunk. It was caught on camera and is a legendary NBA moment.

"

Practice is work. You're working on the idiosyncrasies of what your game needs, so when the game comes, you showcase it and you utilize it. You build your game on it. Practice wasn't just a place to take time off. You work on things in practice. On shooting, on going left or on using your left hand—those types of things that help you get better.

"

On the importance of practice, cigaraficionado.com, August 2005.

Nobody can replace the Doctor. He was the epitome of class and defined the NBA for me. It's a challenge to try and emulate him, but it's not as if I have to go out of my way. Being Michael Jordan means acting the same as I always have.

MJ responds to early comparisons with NBA legend Julius Erving, better known as "Dr. J", *Sports Illustrated*, November 1987.

66

I wonder sometimes myself if it isn't all a dream. I expect to wake up sometime.

99

Pinching himself that it is all really happening, ncaa.com, March 2022.

I Believe I Can Fly...

When I go to church—any church I go to—it doesn't seem like church to me, because everybody stares. I went back to my own church in Wilmington a few times since I've been in the pros, and it really hasn't been the same old church. It's more or less, 'Well, Michael is here today, let's have him speak for us.'

On fame starting to change even the simplest aspects of his life… essentiallysports.com, August 2022.

The Facts #4

Michael Jordan won his first major title at the 1984 Los Angeles Olympic Games, leading the U.S.A. to victory in the final against Spain and winning what would be the first of two Olympic gold medals.

I Believe I Can Fly...

Most of my teammates in Chicago had adapted to
the fans leaving early and just figured, 'The game
must be over.' I'm saying, 'No, it's not over until
there are triple zeros on the scoreboard.' I got a
burst of energy and started to lead the charge.
I got the opportunity to prove it's never really over.
We came from 16 points down to win the game.
That's when the city of Chicago started to say,
'OK, something's starting to happen, something is
changing. There's no give-up in this kid, no matter
what. He's going to keep fighting and fighting and
fighting until we win or lose.' That's how my first
season went. That was the biggest plus for me
when we made the playoffs that year.

On changing the mindset of the Bulls fans,
cigaraficionado.com, August 2005.

"

The scouting report said play me
for the drive, that I couldn't go left.
They didn't know about my first
step or the moves or the jump.
I knew I was taking everybody by
surprise, including myself.

"

On even surprising himself! *Sports Illustrated*,
November 1987.

I never wore a Nike shoe until I signed with Nike. I wore Converse in college, and I was a big Adidas fan. Then Nike came to me about creating my own shoe. They wanted to put my name on my shoe, and [let me] have input into the design of the shoe. I'd never heard of that before. It was a great pitch. It gave me an opportunity to learn more about the shoe industry, and they gave me an opportunity to create.

I sat down with the designers, and I talked to them about my personality and things that I like and things I feel people may like. We put all those thoughts into a brand, into the Jordan brand and the shoe.

99

On creating an iconic shoe, cigaraficionado.com, August 2005.

Chapter 3

#23

*Chicago Bulls' No. 23 had
become the heart and soul of the
team, and a legend was born…*

The Facts #5

Why #23? Michael was inspired as a child by his brother, Larry, who many believe was even better than MJ. They both wore No. 45 jerseys, but when they played on the same high school team, Michael had to pick a new number. He decided to halve 45 and round up to No. 23. It would remain his number for the rest of his playing career.

66

It's not about the shoes, it's what you do in them.

99

An iconic line from an Air Jordans commercial.

#23

66

Oh great, another country boy…

99

MJ's first words to future NBA great Scottie
Pippen, drafted from Arkansas by Chicago Bulls
in 1987, *Michael Jordan: The Life*, Roland Lazenby,
2014.

"

Coach, I'm not gonna let you lose your first game.

"

MJ makes a pledge to new Bulls coach Doug Collins during a fourth quarter time-out… and despite trailing by five points, he is true to his word, inspiring his team to beat the NY Knicks 108–103 at Madison Square Garden in 1987, *Michael Jordan: The Life*, Roland Lazenby, 2014.

#23

> **"**
> I've never seen anything
> like Michael Jordan. Never,
> ever, ever.
> **"**

Doug Collins

The Bulls coach reacts after MJ's incredible 50-point
haul sets a new record at the Garden and wins
the game against the NY Knicks in 1987, *Michael
Jordan: The Life*, Roland Lazenby, 2014

The Facts #6

The most expensive pair of Jordan
sneakers to be sold at retail was the
Jordan 1 collaboration with Dior,
which had a price tag of $2,200 upon
its release in 2020 and has resold
for $12,000.

66

I love 'em right out of the box.
No blisters or anything.

99

On his perfect shoes, *Sports Illustrated*,
November 1987.

The Facts #7

In 1989, the Michael Jordan Foundation began the Michael Jordan Education Club. The Club encouraged youth across the United States to improve their grades and attendance in school and offered the opportunity for students to earn a trip for themselves, a parent, and a teacher to Chicago for a weekend of festivities.

There are plenty of teams in every sport that have great players and never win titles. Most of the time, those players aren't willing to sacrifice for the greater good of the team. The funny thing is, in the end, their unwillingness to sacrifice only makes individual goals more difficult to achieve. One thing I believe to the fullest is that if you think and achieve as a team, the individual accolades will take care of themselves. Talent wins games, but teamwork and intelligence win championships.

On the importance of teamwork, inc.com, April 2016.

"

I think sometimes I'm looked upon as not just a black person but as a person. And I think that's totally new ground for us—and for society. I'm happy to be a pioneer.

"

On breaking new ground as a black athlete, *GQ*, March 1989.

66

You can practice shooting eight
hours a day, but if your technique is
wrong, then all you become is very
good at shooting the wrong way.
Get the fundamentals down and
the level of everything you do
will rise.

99

On refining your technique, tsbasketball.com

66

I would love to own the Chicago Bulls because of what the franchise provided to me. It would give me the opportunity to move it further into a successful program.

99

MJ on his future hopes for the Bulls
cigaraficionado.com, August 2005.

#23

Michael Jordan's support for the Make-A-Wish charity dates back to the first wish he granted in 1989. In the years since then, he has granted hundreds of wishes to children all over the world, becoming one of the all-time most requested celebrity wish-granters. In 2008, he was named Make-A-Wish Chief Wish Ambassador for the life-changing impact he has had on wish kids and their families.

Make-A-Wish America
wish.org.

"

You can't let other people tell you who you are. You have to decide that for yourself.

"

On taking control, exeleonmagazine.com

It's always something I have done. I have robbed a bank. Or I have done cocaine. I have succumbed to the pressures of drugs. I felt the pressure to drink. These are all nightmares. They're nightmares of something terrible happening to me that would destroy a lot of people's dreams or conceptions of me—that's the biggest nightmare I live every day. What if I make a mistake? How might that be viewed?

Everybody feels it's easy to be Michael Jordan with all the good things happening to me, but the things that most scare me are the bad things—the things that would tear down Michael Jordan's image. That's the biggest fear I face. 〞

On his real and imagined nightmares becoming a reality, *GQ*, March 1989.

The Facts #8

Michael Jordan wore a pair of North Carolina practice shorts under his Chicago Bulls shorts for every game.

"

If you're trying to achieve, there will be roadblocks. I've had them; everybody has had them. But obstacles don't have to stop you. If you run into a wall, don't turn around and give up. Figure out how to climb it, go through it, or work around it. **"**

On overcoming obstacles, usab.com
November 2015.

People outside the sport always ask me how old I am. They think I'm 28 or even 30, and in my corporate involvement I try to project myself as that old. In reality, I never want to grow up. I don't know, it's like sometimes I've skipped the years between 24 and 30.

At 30 a guy has to watch what he says, and I'm careful that way. The businesspeople I meet would probably think I'm a jerk if I talked and acted the way I normally do around my friends. And what would my friends think of me in the executive wing?

99

A 24-year-old MJ struggles to balance the pressure with his young age, *Sports Illustrated*, November 1987.

Chapter 4

Air to the Throne

At the peak of his powers,
Michael Jordan ruled the world as
perhaps the most famous sportsman
on the planet, with a Nike partnership
that was well on the way to making
him a billionaire…

Air to the Throne

I can't speak for other people. I have a hard enough time speaking for myself. But if you have a voice, if you have a vision, you have an obligation to speak up.

On finding his voice, exeleonmagazine.com

"

There is no 'I' in 'team,' but there is in 'win.'

"

Characteristically winning words from Jordan's Basketball Hall of Fame induction speech in 2009, speakola.com.

"

I'm not out there sweating for three hours every day just to find out what it feels like to sweat.

"

On putting in the hard graft, tsbasketball.com.

The Facts #9

In 1992, Michael Jordan was a member of the so-called "Dream Team" at the summer Olympics. Alongside Magic Johnson, Larry Bird, Karl Malone, Charles Barkley, Patrick Ewing, Clyde Drexler, Christian Laettner, John Stockton, and his Chicago Bulls teammate Scottie Pippen, Jordan and the U.S. won eight straight games to be crowned the best basketball team in the world, beating Croatia 117–85 in the gold medal clash.

Air to the Throne

"

What the fans on the road come to
see is me get 50 and their
team win.

"

On delivering for the fans, *Sports Illustrated*,
November 1987.

66

Before the 1989–90 season, I married Juanita in the Little White Chapel in Las Vegas in front of a few friends. There was a reason for me getting married and having children. That experience of being a husband and a father provided a balance and a focus away from basketball.

99

On finding balance, *For the Love of the Game: My Story*, 1998.

Air to the Throne

When my first son was born, I felt like I became a man in a sense. There was a new level of maturity. Now I was responsible for that child and for the mother of that child. Not tomorrow or the next day, but every minute of every day. I couldn't think selfishly anymore.

MJ on fatherhood and the life changes and new responsibilities it brought, *For the Love of the Game: My Story*, 1998.

"

During that time they didn't know me as anything but Daddy. They didn't know anything about Michael Jordan the superstar basketball player who did all kinds of endorsement deals. I was a father and a husband. They wouldn't have allowed me to be anything else. That was fine with me.

"

On how becoming a father led to an element of normality at home... *For the Love of the Game: My Story*, 1998.

"

Magic told me he was H.I.V. positive. I was stunned. I couldn't even drive. I pulled off to the side of the road and just listened.

"

MJ receives a call in 1991 from his old friend, Magic Johnson, that knocks him sideways, essentiallysports.com, May 2023.

"

By 1992, I was beginning to feel
like a fish in a fishbowl. My life
was changing, and the way I was
perceived was changing, too.
I was a father and a husband at
home, but everywhere else I was
MICHAEL JORDAN.

"

On the pressures of fame and the effect it was
starting to have on him, *Vanity Fair*, October 1998.

Air to the Throne

As far as being on a pedestal, it's a compliment, yet it's somewhat painful to me that one person can be viewed so high above other people. For example, if I go to a restaurant, I am very likely to get that meal free. But poor people who go to the same restaurant got to wash dishes to eat. And I'm the one that can afford it. If you can explain that, then you can explain society.

Poignant points from MJ, *GQ*, March 1989.

66

Never say never, because limits, like fears, are often just an illusion.

99

Characteristically wise words from Jordan's Basketball Hall of Fame induction speech in 2009, speakola.com

66

Enjoy every minute of life; never second-guess life.

99

Michael Jordan's mantra, thebookofman.com.

"

It's a habit of mine now, noticing labels, logos, shoes. For instance, your sound man, with his Fila jacket and his Reeboks... I haven't said anything to him yet, but I will. **"**

Said with "a wink on his lips", *Sports Illustrated*, November 1987.

Air to the Throne

"

Interviewer: Let's be real. Kids wearing Air Jordans out there on the playground aren't going to turn into Michael Jordans.

Michael Jordan: No, but they'll have the advantage. I tell 'em, the first lesson: Don't be like me. Be better than me. That's the goal.

"

Taken from *Sports Illustrated*, November 1987.

"

You know what he told me? And when he said this, I knew one of us was over the hill. He told me, 'The highest percentage shot on the drive is to lay it up.' He asked me, 'Why do you go on trying those outrageous jumps and moves and dunks?' I couldn't believe it. I just stared at him and said, 'Hey, I don't plan this stuff. It just happens.'

"

Jordan's confusing conversation with a veteran coach, *Sports Illustrated*, November 1987.

> **"**
> Heart is what separates the good from the great. **"**

On how to achieve greatness, inc.com, April 2016.

The Facts #10

Several game-worn sneakers from Michael Jordan's career have sold for incredible amounts of money. The "Flu Game" Jordan XIIs sold for $104,675 at auction in 2013.
An original pair of Jordan 1s that he wore during an exhibition in Italy, which still have a piece of glass in the sole from when he shattered a backboard on a dunk, sold in 2020 for $615,000.

66
Talent wins games, but
teamwork and intelligence win
championships.
99

On how talent isn't enough, forbes.com,
June 2018.

66

Once I made a decision, I never thought about it again.

On being decisive, inc.com, April 2016.

99

The Facts #11

Michael Jordan's highest-scoring game was when he racked up 69 points in a 117–113 overtime win against the Cleveland Cavaliers on March 28, 1990. He scored 60-plus points five times in his career.

66

I've always believed that if you put in the work, the results will come. I don't do things half-heartedly. Because I know if I do, then I can expect half-hearted results.

99

MJ's ethos summed up, cnbc.com, April 2020.

Air to the Throne

I have an older brother, Larry, who has the same heart, the same kind of ability, as I do, and yet he's only five feet eight. This is a guy who will still play me one-on-one in a heartbeat. Despite all I've achieved in basketball, Larry believes he can win. Yet he never got the same opportunities. So I think about that now. Why me?

On his talented brother Larry, *Vanity Fair*, October 1998.

> Larry was so driven and so competitive an athlete that if he had been 6' 2″ instead of 5' 7″, I'm sure Michael would have been known as Larry's brother instead of Larry always being known as Michael's brother.

Pop Herring

Michael and Larry Jordan's high school coach makes quite a statement, biography.com, June 2020.

Air to the Throne

"

The first thing she says, 'You know, you got to be thankful,' and I started looking at the positive. One of the things that he always taught me is that you have to take a negative and turn it into a positive, so I started looking to the other side of it, and that helped me get through it.

"

MJ reflects on how his mother helped him cope with the 1993 murder of his father, James, talksport. com, May 2020.

66

No, because I don't want to know. Because it probably would hurt me even more just to know their reasons. Because if it is, it's going to be totally meaningless for the reasons. It's better that I don't know.

99

MJ reacts to a question of whether he wanted to know his father's killers' motives, people.com, March 2020.

Air to the Throne

I didn't retire because the league kicked me out or they suspended me for a year and a half. That is not true. There's no truth to that. I needed a break. My father just passed. I retired with the notion I wasn't going to come back.

Michael Jordan announced his first retirement in 1993 after the death of his father, *The Last Dance*, Netflix, 2020.

66

People got bored with my skills and what I accomplished was no longer viewed as excellence.

99

MJ expands on reasons not to continue his playing career, slamonline.com.

The Facts #12

Michael Jordan entered Minor League Baseball in 1994 at the age of 31. He played outfield for the Birmingham Barons, a Double-A Minor League affiliate team of the Chicago White Sox, with mixed fortunes.

" Bag it, Michael. "

Sports Illustrated's notorious headline suggesting MJ should give up his attempt at a baseball career, March 1994.

Air to the Throne

SI completely missed the story. Michael Jordan gave up everything he had earned as the king of basketball to play Minor League baseball and subject himself to criticism. He put everything on the line to compete, with nothing to gain. That is the essence of sports. To this day, *SI* has never apologized to Michael, and he'll never talk to them.

David Falk, MJ's agent, on how *Sports Illustrated (SI)* took a cheap shot and perhaps missed a more human angle, mlb.com, April 2020.

"

I'm back.

"

On March 18, 1995, Michael Jordan shocks the world when he returns to basketball and resumes his NBA career with Chicago Bulls. He shared the news with two simple words! nba.com, March 2020.

"

The game is my wife. It demands loyalty and responsibility, and it gives me back fulfilment and peace. **"**

On his relationship with the sport, tsbasketball.com.

The Facts #13

The only time Michael Jordan wore the number 45 after committing to 23 was after the return from his first retirement in March 1995. He finished out the regular season and the first round of the playoffs in the new number before struggling in Game 1 of the Eastern Conference semifinals and deciding he had better luck in No. 23.

Chapter 5

Family, Friends, and Inspirations

Michael Jordan has inspired
so many people during his career.

Here, his family, friends, fellow
celebrities, and opponents share
what MJ means to them...

The Facts #14

In 1996, Michael Jordan played himself in the live action/animated sports comedy movie Space Jam. It was a huge hit, and further cemented MJ's celebrity.

"

For me? Michael Jordan, Michael Jackson, and Beyoncé are the three greatest entertainers of my lifetime; and you could probably throw Muhammad Ali in there.

"

Magic Johnson

The NBA legend names the people that have given him most joy, X post, April 2020.

Family, Friends, and Inspirations

Getting a text from Michael Jordan today, that's... I'm a big Jordan guy my whole life. I was a little kid in Iowa saving 100 bucks for a pair of Jordans back in the day. Pretty darn cool, to say the least. **99**

Michael Block

The PGA Championship winner reveals a text from his hero completed a dream come true, golf.com, May 2023.

"

If you don't know how to play fast, then you are not allowed to come back. With him, if you don't play fast, he will leave you. He's a competitor. That's the other thing, you get to see guys as a competitor in golf, and you've gotta compete because you're with the best, and when you compete with him, you've gotta bring your A-game.

"

Jason Kidd

The NBA coach and former Dallas Mavericks and Phoenix Suns star outlines MJ's fierce style and competitive nature, golf.com, June 2021.

Family, Friends, and Inspirations

Michael was such a superstar in the game of basketball, and he was a bigger superstar than any sport had ever had. It wasn't like he was any average guy and like, 'Let's go have lunch.' It's different. My rookie year he gave me a pair of golf clubs. He was trying to lure me in so he could take all my money!

Scottie Pippen

Former Chicago Bulls teammate shares his memories of MJ, golf.com, April 2020.

66

He'll play you for whatever you want. Whatever makes you scared.

99

Rickie Fowler

The U.S. golf star shares a glimpse of the gambling-loving MJ, essentiallysports.com, November 2021.

We roll around another 18 and I take him for another couple [thousand dollars]. Now we've been drinking all afternoon and he's going from Sunset Ridge to the stadium, to play a game. I'm messing around. I'm like, 'I'm gonna call my bookie. All the money you just lost to me, I'm putting on Cleveland [to beat the Bulls].'

He goes, 'I'll tell you what. I'll bet you that we'll win by 20 points, and I have more than 40 [points].' I'm like, 'Done.' Son of a gun goes out and scores 52 and they win by 26 points or something.

"

Jeremy Roenick

The NHL legend gets sucked in by the Jordan wagering machine, golf.com, January 2020

The thing about Michael that you all need to understand is that he doesn't worry about what you all think of him.

Charles Barkley

On Michael's attitude, *Sports Illustrated*, February 2013.

"
I know fear is an obstacle for some people, but it is an illusion to me. Failure always made me try harder next time.

"

Michael on overcoming fear, inc.com, April 2016.

Family, Friends, and Inspirations

In the age of TV sports, if you were to create a media athlete and star for the '90s—spectacular talent, midsized, well-spoken, attractive, accessible, old-time values, wholesome, clean, natural, not too Goody Two-Shoes, with a little bit of deviltry in him—you'd invent Michael. He's the first modern crossover in team sports. We think he transcends race, transcends basketball.

David Falk

MJ's long-time agent succinctly describes his superstar client, *Sports Illustrated*, November 1987.

"

I always told my children, 'Each one of you has special gifts, it's how you use them.' Each one had a talent, but how they approached it was different from the others. Michael might have skills for basketball, but Larry built things with his hands, and our oldest son was in ROTC and such a leader.

"

Deloris Jordan

Michael's mom is proud of all her kids no matter what, people.com, April 2023.

Family, Friends, and Inspirations

My career is totally different than Michael Jordan's. What I've gone through is totally different than what he went through. What he did was unbelievable, and I watched it unfold. I looked up to him so much. I think it's cool to put myself in a position to be one of those great players, but if I can ever put myself in a position to be the greatest player, that would be something extraordinary.

LeBron James

Paying homage to MJ, basketballnetwork.com, March 2024.

"

Michael has a different burden than any other player in the NBA, and personally, I do not know how he can keep up his energy and his night-in, night-out performance, with all the things he's had thrown at him. I mean, the guy is a phenomenal athlete, but he's also a phenomenal person to deal with—he's a very sensitive, caring young man, very, very loyal to his friends. And I always ask myself: If I were 25 right now and had what Michael Jordan has, could I deal with it? And I'm not sure that I could. That's the thing about him I respect so much.

"

Doug Collins

The Bulls' coach in awe of MJ, *GQ*, March 1989.

Family, Friends, and Inspirations

He would try to get me to play golf all the time. Mike, I know about you. I've written book reports about you in elementary school. I know you started playing golf in North Carolina. So that means if I'm doing the math, you've been playing golf for like a hundred years. I have not picked up a golf club ever. The last thing you're going to do is get me on a golf course and annihilate me. Not gonna do it.

Kobe Bryant

The late and much-loved NBA legend stays ahead of the game with his old (and occasionally conniving!) friend and stays away from the greens, sportsillustrated.com, September 2023.

"

What you get from me is from him.
I don't get five championships here
without him.

"

Kobe Bryant
A heartfelt tribute to MJ, gq.com, May 2020.

Family, Friends, and Inspirations

I didn't think it was real, man. You don't understand. I didn't think Michael Jordan was real. I only thought he lived in the TV. When I saw him, I was like, if the man above would have taken me that day, I would've lived a hell of a life, I swear to God.

LeBron James

Recounting his first meeting with the legend that lived inside the TV, people.com, January 2024.

"

Michael Jordan was my… everyone wanted to be like Mike, so like, even when I see Mike today, I'm still like, 'That's Michael Jordan right there,' you know. And I just think he's the coolest guy and you know I love his determination.

"

Tom Brady

The NFL legend reveals the inspiration behind his own achievements, thesportsrush.com, September 2023.

66

I always look at a negative and turn it into a positive.

99

On finding the positive, sportsforthesoul.com, June 2020.

66

I can accept failure, everyone fails at something. But I can't accept not trying.

On the importance of trying, medium.com, May 2020.

99

He remembers everyone who ever didn't think he was going to be great… He remembers every negative story that's ever been written about him.

Jerry Krause

The former Bulls general manager outlines how MJ used negativity as a driving force throughout his career, espn.com, January 2024.

All the attention is well deserved. We're talking about a guy who's playing basketball over the last two years like I've never seen played.

Isiah Thomas

Detroit Pistons and former NBA champion praises MJ, GQ, March 1989.

"

We had a lot of athletes on the show, but Jordan was the pinnacle.

"

Robert Smigel

The *Saturday Night Live* writer on MJ's legendary appearances on the long-running sketch show, slamonline.com, June 2020.

66

He was the biggest star that had ever done the show… He was at the height of his powers. It was like hanging around Iron Man or something.

99

Chris Rock

On his *SNL* appearance with MJ, slamonline.com, June 2020.

Family, Friends, and Inspirations

"

The cast is used to famous people—we had famous people on every week, and nobody would ask for autographs or anything. But Jordan, yo… it got to the point, they had to put a guard, a policeman, outside Michael Jordan's dressing room for the cast. Just for us.

"

Chris Rock

More on MJ's legendary status, slamonline.com, June 2020.

66

If you do the work, you get
rewarded. There are no shortcuts
in life.

99

Michael Jordan's inspirational attitude, inc.com,
April 2016.

"

He was hanging out, we became tight—for the week, you know. He was genuinely lovable. He was just cool, man. Handsome dude. He owned the whole place.

"

Adan Sandler

MJ recruits another devoted fan during his *SNL* stints, slamonline.com, June 2020.

66

We all were in love with him. He
was the greatest. It was like the
Jordan you loved when he hits
a shot and smiles—that's who we
had on the show.

99

Adan Sandler

One legend, on another, MJ, slamonline.com,
June 2020.

Family, Friends, and Inspirations

It was Godly. I've said that over and over before, but it was like meeting God for the first time. That's what I felt like as a 16-year-old kid when I met MJ.

LeBron James

On meeting his idol, espn.com, December 2018.

"

I'm not so sure Michael's not one of the better defensive players in basketball. He doesn't hound you to death. He's just got so much athletic ability, he can cover anybody.

"

Jerry Sloan

The former Bulls defender praises one of the supposed weaker sides of MJ's game, sportsillustrated.com, January 2024.

Family, Friends, and Inspirations

"

I played a couple of times with Michael Jordan, and I remember being a fool once and accepting one of his bets on a putt. He wanted to make it some crazy amount—in the thousands. I'm not a big gambler. I lined up the putt and, over and over, Jordan starts ripping the Velcro on his golf glove.

I was like, 'What are you doing?!' And he goes, 'Look, man. If I can make a free throw with 20,000 people screaming at me, you can make a putt with me making a little noise.'

"

Michael Douglas

The latest to suffer one of MJ's famous 'wagers' on the green, golf.com, June 2021.

Family, Friends, and Inspirations

I thought in the early days, he was doing so much, it was unbelievable. He always visited with some person or child who had a last wish. He never turned anyone down. Every night he faced that, and I could never understand how he was strong enough to do it. I can still remember he saw a kid who was brought in whose father had burned his face off him. They brought him in, and Michael talked to him in that old dressing room we had in Chicago Stadium before the game. He just talked to him.

You couldn't imagine, a kid that was hideously burned. And Michael just talked to him. He put him on the bench, and during the game he would come over and ask, 'How'd you like that jump shot?' One of the officials came over and said, 'Michael, you can't have that kid on the bench. It's against league rules.' And Michael looked at him and said, 'He's on the bench.'

Johnny Bach

Former assistant Bulls coach shares his memories of MJ... and his incredible work ethic on and off the court, basketballnetwork.com, October 2019.

Family, Friends, and Inspirations

"

I used to eat and drink anything I wanted. Because of how active I was, I could get away with it. Once you get out of the daily routine of physical activity, you settle into a normal routine. It becomes harder to say no to a cheeseburger!

"

Even the GOAT has to watch his waistline these days! Gq.com, May 2020.

"

I was thinking, at first, I might be a little somewhat nervous about it, but then I realized I'm not going to be nervous about showing emotions for someone I absolutely loved. That's the humanistic side of me—people tend to forget I do have one.

"

MJ's heartfelt tribute to Kobe Bryant following his tragic death in a helicopter crash, as quoted on espn.com, August 2021.

Chapter 6

The GOAT

The Greatest of All Time debate
will rage in basketball as it
does in every sport, but here are
some Michael Jordan quotes
that might sway the argument
his way...

I think he's God disguised as Michael Jordan. He is the most awesome player in the NBA. Today in Boston Garden, on national TV, in the playoffs, he put on one of the greatest shows of all time. I couldn't believe someone could do that against the Boston Celtics. **99**

Larry Bird

The legendary Boston Celtics forward's famous commentary line after a Jordan supershow on April 21, 1986, talksport.com, October 2024.

"

[Muhammad Ali] crossed many barriers, many lines. He was a pioneer in the sense to see these people viewed as people instead of their race or color or whatever, and I think this is my ultimate goal, to be viewed as a person first, and even though my race is black, that I am a person just like you and any other person.

"

From one GOAT to another, MJ's reverence to boxing legend Ali was clear on Australian TV in 1993, sportskeeda.com, July 2023.

NBA Honors

Six-time NBA champion
1991, 1992, 1993, 1996, 1997, 1998

Six-time NBA Finals MVP
1991, 1992, 1993, 1996, 1997, 1998

Five-time NBA MVP
1988, 1991, 1992, 1996, 1998

NBA Defensive Player of the Year
1987–88

NBA Rookie of the Year
1984–85

10-time NBA scoring leader
1987–1993, 1996–1998

Three-time NBA steals leader
1988, 1990, 1993

14-time NBA All-Star
1985–1993, 1996–1998, 2002, 2003

Three-time NBA All-Star Game MVP
1988, 1996, 1998

10-time All-NBA First Team
1987–1993, 1996–1998

One-time All-NBA Second Team
1985

Nine-time NBA All-Defensive First Team
1988–1993, 1996–1998

NBA All-Rookie First Team
1985

Two-time NBA Slam Dunk Contest champion
1987, 1988

Two-time IBM Award winner
1985, 1989

**Named one of the 50 Greatest Players
in NBA History**
1996

**Selected on
the NBA 75th Anniversary Team**
2021

I've missed more than 9,000 shots in my career. I've lost almost 300 games. Twenty-six times I've been trusted to take the game-winning shot and missed. I've failed over and over and over again in my life. And that is why I succeed.

Michael Jordan
Never afraid to try, forbes.com.

"

I'm going to have to say Michael Jordan because Michael paved the way for all the great guys that we have now. And 6–0 in the Finals without a legitimate big man. Went through a lot. Took a year off. Came back and won three in a row. He's definitely the greatest player.

"

Shaquille O'Neal

NBA giant delivers his GOAT verdict, bleacherreport.com, May 2020.

Everybody always says it's me and Larry [Bird]. Really, it's Mike and everybody else.

Magic Johnson

His verdict on the GOAT debate, msn.com.

Honors and Achievements

No. 23 retired by the Chicago Bulls

No. 23 retired by the Miami Heat

Chicago Bulls Ring of Honor

NBA MVP trophy renamed in Jordan's honor
("Michael Jordan Trophy") in 2022

Two-time Olympic gold medal winner
1984, 1992

Tournament of the Americas gold medal winner
1992

Pan American Games gold medal winner
1983

Two-time U.S.A. Basketball Male Athlete of the Year
1983, 1984

66

He's easily the best practice player
I've seen in my life.

99

Doug Collins

The former Chicago Bulls coach on MJ's legendary
practice sessions, and his preference not to come
out for pregame shoot-rounds because, "I want to
be hitting the court for the first time, fresh" as MJ
put it, *Sports Illustrated*, November 1987.

"

As you get older, you look back,
and you understand how you
became the person you are. I don't
think I would be here without the
lessons that I learned at a very
young age. That competitiveness
within me started when I was
a kid

"

MJ traces back where the seeds of determination
to succeed were first planted, Netflix's *The Last
Dance*, 2020.

Michael Jordan has overcome
the acceleration of gravity by the
application of his muscle power in
the vertical plane, thus producing a
low-altitude earth orbit.

Lieutenant Colonel Douglas Kirkpatrick
Department of Astronautics, U.S. Air Force Academy,
GQ, March 1989.

"

Basketball legend Michael Jordan proves that it is better to give than to receive by making a record-setting donation of $10 million to Make-A-Wish America in honor of his 60th birthday on Feb. 17. The gift—the largest from an individual in the organization's 43-year history—is Jordan's latest show of commitment to the wish-granting organization that he has actively supported for more than 30 years.

"

Make-A-Wish America

wish.org, February 2023.

66

For the past 34 years, it's been an honor to partner with Make-A-Wish and help bring a smile and happiness to so many kids. Witnessing their strength and resilience during such a tough time in their lives has truly been an inspiration.

99

On supporting the Make-A-Wish foundation, nba.com, February 2023.

The Facts #15

Michael Jordan was inducted into the Naismith Memorial Basketball Hall of Fame in 2009. He chose his childhood hero, former North Carolina State star David Thompson, to present him.

The GOAT

When Michael Jordan arrived in Chicago in 1984, a skinny kid with a full head of hair and a winning smile, everyone knew he was going to be good. After all, here was a player who, as a freshman, had hit the game-winning shot to propel the North Carolina Tar Heels over the Georgetown Hoyas in a national championship game, and had gone on to be a two-time first team All-American, an Olympic gold medal winner, and a national player of the year.

What people didn't realize at the time—
what maybe even Michael didn't realize
at the time—was that the same young
man would become the greatest player
the game had ever seen, a transcendent
athlete who would fundamentally change
the face of sports, commerce and
American culture.

"

Barack Obama

The former U.S. President's tribute to His Airness,
sportsillustrated.com, January 2024.

66

Everybody has talent, but ability takes hard work.

99

On working for your dreams, thebookofman.com.

The Facts #16

In 2020, The Last Dance was released on Netflix, a documentary that charted Jordan's career. A critical and commercial success, it also put Jordan back at the centre of public consciousness.

The minute you get away from fundamentals—whether its proper technique, work ethic, or mental preparation—the bottom can fall out of your game, your schoolwork, your job, whatever you're doing.

More on perfecting those fundamentals, bleacherreport.com, February 2013.

"

Some people want it to happen,
some wish it would happen, and
others make it happen.

"

On not assuming anything will come to you,
medium.com, February 2017.

"

Congratulations to LeBron on this incredible achievement. It's a testament to his hard work, longevity, and his great skill.

"

Michael Jordan's praise after LeBron passes Kareem Abdul-Jabbar's NBA points record, mirror.co.uk, February 2023.

66

He's a heck of a basketball player, without a doubt.

99

On another potential GOAT, LeBron, nytimes.com, January 2020.

❝

I play to win, whether during practice or a real game, and I will not let anything get in the way of me and my competitive enthusiasm to win.

❞

On his winning mentality, 247sports.com.

"

I listened, I was aware of my success, but I never stopped trying to get better.

"

For the Love of the Game: My Story, 1998.

In some ways, Kobe was self-made. People forget that. He was an 18-year-old kid that made himself into one of the best. To me, it was all from hard work and dedication. All the effort he put forth. He should be a great role model for a lot of kids who at 18 may not want to go to college, that may want to play basketball somewhere.

He showed them how. And he sat on the bench for a long time before he got his chance. People forget that, too. But when he got his shot, he took advantage of it. "

MJ's touching tribute to Kobe Bryant, outlining the legacy his close friend left behind and how that can inspire kids from similar backgrounds, espn.com, May 2021.

"

Retirement means you can design and choose your moment. I can design shoes one day and ski the next... That is how I am going to live.

"

On finding ways to fill his days, *Vanity Fair*, October 1998.

66

I've never lost a game; I just ran out of time.

99

On never giving up, thesportsrush.com, January 2021.

❝

You're never going to say who's the greatest of all time. To me, that's more for PR and more for selling stories. I never played with Wilt Chamberlain or Jerry West so to say one is greater than the other is being unfair

❞

MJ isn't even willing to discuss being the GOAT, thesportsrush.com, October 2020.

---

66 If it turns out that my best wasn't good enough, at least I won't look back and say I was afraid to try. **99**

On the importance of trying over anything else, on3.com, April 2022.

The GOAT

When I'm on my game, I don't think there's anybody that can stop me… Once I get the ball, you're at my mercy. There's nothing you can say or do about it. I own the ball, I own the game.

"

Michael Jordan's acknowledges his own relentless playing style, *GQ*, March 1989.